Some of You Will Know

ARROWSMITH
PRESS

Also by David Rivard:

Standoff

Otherwise Elsewhere

Sugartown

Bewitched Playground

Wise Poison

Torque

Some of You Will Know

Poems by David Rivard

Some of You Will Know
David Rivard

ISBN: 979-8-9863401-0-4

Boston — New York — San Francisco — Baghdad
San Juan — Kyiv — Istanbul — Santiago, Chile
Beijing — Paris — London — Cairo — Madrid
Milan — Melbourne — Jerusalem — Darfur

11 Chestnut St.
Medford, MA 02155

arrowsmithpress@gmail.com
www.arrowsmithpress.com

The Forty-Third Arrowsmith book was typeset & designed by Ezra Fox
for Askold Melnyczuk & Alex Johnson in Palatino font

Cover art by Jeesoo Lee:
One Page, Two Stories

for Amy

CONTENTS

And that's all I asked for was a clue.

—*James Tate*

You Say You Don't Know

I say I
don't know what's
wrong with me,
but of course
I do. Like the shadows
of sunflowers
stuck in themselves
at noon. Stalled.
Waiting. Ten thousand words
on the tip of my tongue,
ten thousand lives
leaning against the lightning-lit
fence post. The wood
charred. Struck. Smoking.
Electricity licks the soles
of our feet even now, the earth loves us
even when we can't
love ourselves.
You all,
all of you
say you don't know
what's wrong
with you, but
of course you do,
you have to.

Open Secret

A starling
wades in a wide bowl in the garden,
the water cooled by the bowl's thick stone
dark & clean & earthly
like water that dried mushrooms have soaked in,
a calming, almost
personal transparency that coats the bird's feathers
and that she takes with her to a branch,
where she shakes her short, square-tipped tail
and flies off inside a spray
of iridescent droplets in the noonish air,
'each drop a petty tricolor'
in the solstice heat building out of June,
that moment of July

when a video of the long line
of refrigerated freight cars
stacked with black body bags
in an insurgent-controlled Ukrainian
train depot surfaces
in the newsfeed all of a sudden, on that sunny, bacon-fat
morning two days after the otherwise intangible day
an airliner full of human bodies
disintegrates at altitude
in the sky
over cornfields and sunflowers
in the Donetsk Oblast.

The starling doesn't use words.
She offers no indictment or consolation, no answer:
just resting—flying off—

only immersion
in the available
atmosphere or solution,
whether shimmering, cool water
or air full of pagan heat.

The investigators wear haz-mat suits
of white Tyvek & goggles
dark & shiny as the pupils of salmon
buried to their chins in crushed ice.

A single heartbeat
one heartbeat ends the past
and begins
the future.

Pond

You aren't the first to feel these things—
       or are you? would you like to have been?
you whose loneliness became you
       if you thought yourself the first
would it change you? (I bet that
       you would like to be changed) humbled
by being chosen reborn
       would you even know you'd been
reborn (I think you would) after all
       you'd woken helmetless last night
again & again before the sun returned
       the sun as usual bristling a little then
don't deny the gift of happiness don't
       think it's meaningless even if it fades
it would still take a paintbrush made
       entirely of the thickest of eyelashes
to get it on canvas that face of yours
       as it emerged a minute ago warming up
without warning near the end of June
       a kind of 19th century face
with high Gallic cheekbones & watchful eyes
       under a straw hat wide-brimmed
its tan crown banded by black ribbon
       your eyes shaded by the brim
you studied the effects then of the drink
       taken in long sips from that hip flask
a tree carries as it walks through winter & spring
       early spring slow sips imperceptible
wild traceries of green at the tips of
       poplars & willows their elixirs

turn the water to fluorescent algae
near the shore now that the thousands of
polliwogs & minnows feed on it too
the lip of the pond overfull
after last night's torrent someone's cheap
wristwatch left on a canvas lawn chair
in a netted cup-holder the sweat-dark
strap evidence of the body missing
from this scene but loved for its pulse
the watch still ticking after all that
lightning rain & thunder so many hours
have to pass for all the faces it takes
so long to see hooded within a face
loneliness is such a dark cloak
it doesn't reveal itself so easily
it wavers there below you
on the sandy bottom as you float
under rushing clouds almost
dead center of the pond your shadow
a cloak dark & cold as your shame
warm & dark as your freedom.

The City from Which We Have Travelled

A little ruthless—
blue & white buses pass by
on their way to Longwood Medical Center,
where the entire world
will wind up one day for sure—

someplace like it
anyway—a deathbed pallet in arboreal Guinea Bissau,
or the infirmary at a mining camp
in tungsten Kazakhstan,
or palliative hospice care
in your 40-year, mortgage-free home—
if you're lucky, *you* might die
in your split-level ranch, a quarter-acre tied-up
on the Braintree/Milton line—

just like that: gone.

In the meantime, once-in-awhile,
there I stood on the Pont Neuf,
less than an ounce of nationalistic envy & inferiority
in total body weight,
face forward at sunset, wiped almost clean
in the aroused jet lag of having lost track of the fact
that I'm an American,
carried away by the flat-bottomed boats below—

meanwhile my sister had tied around her neck
a batik scarf
and eaten the grassy meat of a blind Indonesian goat
and heard the rooster

crowing morning into the village without anvils
while the last few minutes of the *wayang kulit* spooled out;
and she believed that
as the puppet gods of the shadow theater live limitless
inside space & time they must have
been watching her all her life, even when she was 14,
when she would touch her hand to her little sweater breasts
in the mall Cineplex, the house lights having dimmed,
the air conditioning kicking on—

we can go on because we can forget, it's true—

just as our mother told us—the engine of all this
herself—she who was able once
to sail a small sloop solo
across the Great Lakes,
through the Erie Canal, & into the Hudson
down to New York—
who, when she talked of it later to her children,
could make it sound as easy almost
as casual & full of routine
as a long, long trolley ride
across the city where we lived, the textile mills
in that town granite-walled, & the weaving
sheds with their tall looms
banging out a stiff racket, the clatter
of the shuttles, recoiling belts, & conveyors
terrible & hot—

there in that insolid city,
the home from which all of us have travelled so far,
on an errand we can no longer recall.

Spit

Some progress is anything but.

And my country is cold now, even if the roses are not.

And I would be stateless today, all for the sake of self-respect.

Listen to all those
hard-living shouters as they sing—
most of them blue jays
so on the outs
they could have died just before dawn
had they been born
in Hank Williams' car,
tho they might
just as well have been gamblers
in a steamboat rain,
if not electrons shuffling pointlessly
through the brain's
necrotizing cells—

most of them blue jays, but not this one...

this shouter of creole...this
Haitian a man
who in the ancient world would have been called
"an unfortunate,"
his arms wind-milling like a conductor, a homeless
conductor of meatpacker's music
as he rides down the street on frightening voices
and all his damaged resources
just out of the picture

while shaking his fist at the homes he passes—

my house, my neighbors'—

and something lumpish
growing there on the back
of his shaved head, right at the neck—
a mud dauber's nest,
or an impacted meteor from one of the lousier quadrants,
a soft peach he slept on....

god, all this language,
it wipes out the world & its pain
with words
it so often wants
likeness to wash through
consolation as such.

I say I hear, but do I see?

What's the point of our surveillance apparatus
if not to save the lives of the desperate.

"He rubbed spit on the blind one's eyes,"
wrote the recorder of miracles, "spit & clay."
So the blind one could see.

The Wish of Those Who Named Us

There is the question of
bearing witness, of being yourself seen
by yourself, & seen clearly, cleanly,
without weapon or bible in hand;
as this was the wish,
the sturdy & not-so-secret wish
of those who named us—

our parents wanted us to be
known to ourselves without confusion:
without judgment,
sans suffering. Never force it,
they said, always find it.

OK, strictly speaking, that's not entirely true.
My particular, sole, insistent, moody mother & father
probably never thought much about it at all.
Those two anxious citizens,
they were never exemplars of patience.
The weightlessness of detachment & acceptance
as I think of it now
would have frightened them—
for good reason.

If you could see these words
I'm speaking to you tonight printed on a page
as typeface & magnified x 500
you would feel just how ragged & coarse
they really are, heavy—

well, playing the part of a butterfly
must be tiring, right?
I'm happier being the old ox, right?

On some plane of existence
these two scraps are all my news:
where the mess is
that's where my heart is.

Seeker

It's not lonely along the river Taunton
but it is windy with the second cousin of loneliness,
distance—at sunset
when they appear there suddenly
independent of dusk
the clouds want just as fast to sneak away—

upright is a good word
for how you might feel in that place as a child,
upright but teetering
between bouts of
freeze tag & milk room gossip.
Your parents would have told you
at one time or another to live like the coldest
of skate blades—*stand on you own,*
take care of yourself, stay
sharp. "Watch where you're going,"
your mother's constant warning.

You thought
she meant *race away, little skate, hurry, hurry—*
but when you did, it surprised you
how hurt she was.

Hadn't you been afraid all along
of how heartless
it might be to become an adult?

Did I mention the dream,
the one no one by the river remembers yet
of the day the terracotta soldiers

began to breathe—tall as the first
Chinese emperor, stiff at the elbows
from cold years in the tomb, nearly Rastafarian
in their stoned ferocity & leather headgear,
they were on the hunt. And then there was the girl—
it was on me to help this young girl get away.
She stood in the middle of a field of tall wheat,
balanced on one leg, chin up. A child's way
of escaping, a wish. A cottage was offered to us, a refuge
set quietly amid the strange improbability
of all those neon signs blinking by the sea,
a boardwalk town at end of season.
But I refused the house. We stole a sailboat
from the harbor.
                        Do you think it possible
to forgive yourself? As a boy I'd believed
that a paper boat was immune
to gravity & water. Such a boat could not be sunk.
I could always sail it home.
Did I think that more than anything
what this girl wanted
was to be instructed by the sea?
To learn...what? Wildness?
Yes. Wildness—
which is what wonder & wiseness feel like
to the homesick.

Trophy

I believed a secret
keyhole might be found
in each & every city

And somewhere
were the keys to the city—
kept in a cluttered kitchen drawer,
not quite forgotten
but somehow gone missing

Many times now
I've seen myself the way
my mother saw me

"No disguises
in dreams," that's what she
would say

I sit at my desk
and complicate all
that has happened since
my mother looked
at my face & told me
that one day I'd be glad
I'd inherited her skin—
until, after a while,
something out there
or something here
inside me says, no, stop it
you should just write—
and that's
what I do

What a thought—it
sounds almost childish, so
simple, as if the sun
had given itself
a trophy when a warbler
flew from a tree,
and the bird
was the trophy itself

Without disguise
the stag appeared
one evening, as if
it had earned the right
only because of how cold & green
the ocean is as it flows
through the late summer meadow
a moment or at most two
for the grasses parted
by a North Atlantic wind

The Clock

Life goes fast, doesn't it?—
I mean, *really*—
full of dopamine & dumbass shouting—
like a boxing ring at an Amvets post
on the south side, the fifth bout of
a six-fight smoker, where a club fighter
in bright red & gold silks sits between rounds
the split swollen above his right eyebrow
being stitched, a woman ringside
in dark angora hoodie
watching the needle do its work—
his girlfriend—taller than he is—
the countergirl at an auto parts store,
her nails shaped & lacquered
with coy gold crosses
neither goth nor christian—
and it is always mostly true
that she's the one who feels herself
at the center of the picture—
her dead father is always inside her,
her mother adrift
in some elusive, far-off city or forest
20 years after ditching her husband & kid.
Above the bed this auto parts clerk slept in
as a child hung a clock
in the shape of a cat, a black & white tuxedo
whose eyes swung back & forth
as it kept time,
its attention unwavering,
the clock's hands circling its stomach,
its curled black tail

swishing back & forth to the ticking—
a cat oddly unfazed
by all the time it had swallowed.
To think of that cat
makes her feel neat & clean even now—
it looked so
clever, so capable, & almost kindly,
almost as if it were ready
just about bursting
to wish everyone who glanced its way
good luck.

15 Minutes

Fine, the clock
then—the one in the diner,
for god's sake!

Because how long would it take
and why would I
want to stop gluing these feathers together
and calling it a bird
if it sings
what I'd made as a matter of fact
with my mind—my own mind—the mind
so often
working working working
on a chain gang. Why should I
stop? This bird sings.

I don't know,
the whole thing makes you wonder.
Jesus. It really does.

We're all such *people*,
each of us expanding at the same
speed as the universe—
I mean it, just people.

So weren't there a million
worried looks
I cast at the clock? The clock first,
and then the waitress, the schlubby one
who kept addressing the other
waitress—the more resourceful,

more amiable waitress—
as "Happy Bunny." Each of us looking
to spend as much time as we could
with the untidy winds
that come from down south.

Those winds wish us to be warm,
they want only
to credential-check the snow,
because sleep...
a long, deep, Ozarks-style nap...
sleep beats
the hell out of the grave,
the grave & all
its defensiveness.

The Sentence

Like a 5-hour visit to a thrift shop,
that's how my day is going—
poking around the bargain bins for those soft cloth booties
worn in hospital operating rooms,
the kind that are rubber-soled for grip
and quiet
so as not to disturb or keep either patient or surgeon
from their meeting with fate, the nursing team
trying hard not to scare away
the skittish, hog-eyed, much-rumored hope of healing.

I'm a sensitive soul—
I say that, & everybody laughs,
but I over-react to nearly everything.

That's always been my problem.

My brain is a single, small part
of a heavy-duty anxiety machine, a thick bolt in a turbine blade
humping nonstop in the midst of a skyline-jamming wind farm.

It's my go-to option, my real job.

*

Mostly there's a lot of moonlighting in this life—
tho they call it *a career*—a career, the long workweek we all
have to spend on an enclosure gang, hammer in hand.

So the women who once drew
with radium green paint

the luminescent numbers 1 through 12 on alarm clock faces
would sharpen the tips of their sable brushes
by licking them, absentmindedly,
and 20 years later were dead,
cancers of the lip, cancers of the mouth & throat.

So the honeybee realizes the meaning
of the flowering rosemary with its soft buzzing.

And the rosemary bush
gets the gist of the honeybee too—
it quivers slightly,
shaking with a sort of laughter.

That's right, & we can actually
be packed with all our usernames & passwords
into the barrel of a pistol,
and shot out
like a single, burning bullet,
without even knowing it—
that's about the size of it, that & the 6,000
feet of air that you rip through.

*

There was this fellow I knew once—
a putz, but mean—a cardsharp with circulation issues
in his fingertips, a wannabe bottom dealer—
after a leap year full of short-circuits
he'd returned to the homeland that he'd emigrated from—
then a decade or so later
one night he turned up without warning
on my cable newsfeed,
one of those gold-necklaced cutthroats loitering

on the roadside with an automatic rifle, staring dull-eyed
at a house on fire near the outskirts of Donetsk.

"When you
achieve enlightenment," he used to tell me,
"I will send my greeting
to you. 'Fuck you,'
is what it will say.
With cheerful affection."

The digitalized smoke behind him not unlike
the smoke in an old, hand-tinted wirephoto:
a haze rising 500 feet above the walled compound
set aflame by one warlord or another.

*

Skin, hair, hide, pelt,
all these surfaces we wear like costumes
weigh us down, a sluggishness
just when we're ready to escape,
right as we're about to take a shortcut
across a wide expanse of mown green lawn,
the solar grasses of an old cemetery.

Hey, there's Noah & Amy
standing over by Bob's grave. There's me,
touching the letters that run down the back,
a sentence carved in granite —
the stone doesn't say what crimes
this sentence was passed in judgment of—
the crimes of a man guilty
of friendship, guilty of
frustration, bitterness (so be it) running off

to good times, talk with children
lost to worries, distracted loves, quizzical changes,
air sickness, lots of laughter, fine tuning,
and / or squinting—a little lovesick,
that would be my guess,
Bob being who Bob seemed to be that is.

"Look at the light of this hour"—
that's what the sentence reads.

Look at the light of this hour.

Bronte Shoreline

"I don't
know why I stay
with you," you said.
Hard rain had taken
a hammer to
the wings of our bird
before waking—
a white-throated
sparrow—it felt criminal
because guilty—guilty of
what? space
and time & dirt?
moss carried-off
through rain
to a swallow's nest? I felt
snow on my thighs,
pants soaked
after I fell asleep last July
only to wake
on the street this December
at the moment I stood there alone
side-by-side
of all those commuters
looking bored by intention
as they waited for the bus,
above their woolen heads
the plexiglass roof of the kiosk
curled like a wave.
Likewise we will both
be for walking soon
by a Bronte shoreline,

the windswept mist
saving face
but the two of us lost
to each other
inside it for however long
it wants.

Solar Cycle

In our Xmas tree ornaments
the reflected lights are green & red LEDs flickering—
vexed by the drying
sprigs of bluish pine needles.
A scotch pine in an Inman Square sun-parlor
is a utopian forest tract
urbanized in miniature, room bound,
the street that runs outside the windows plowed
only vaguely
after morning sleet & snow.
The solar cycle never betrays us,
it's happening as & when we meet:
constant friend, peeved mortal enemy—
but the rock-ribbed sun this December 27th
has asked to be
reincarnated as a small, ragged mole
just below the shave line
of my beard—
touch it, Baby Snooks, rub it hard,
be lucid
as the Nativity approaches,
then fades—
lope along!
Got it?
A crow stands alone
under the milky sun, not in heaven yet.
Is Tomaž's soul back now
in its old haven,
a strongbox?—'great poets'
foretell their own death in a single line.'
Bare flurries, barely

snowing at all—bits of
clear water in a brilliant mood frozen
amid all the *agita*
and apeshit. A strongbox in heaven
is a shoebox here,
the cardboard box into which
Tomaž had once laid a dead rabbit—
his hands trembled, he told me,
when he let go of the cold fur,
the furiously cold pelt
of that rich animal
he'd killed totally by accident.

—in memory of Tomaž Šalamun

Walk Me Out

Inside of this accidentally
on purpose caught I know
in my heart it is morning
dew on my loafers that
wets me when I have
something to say I have
never heard because
I haven't had a chance yet
to say it. Not yet.
There are certain eyes
you cannot fool, extreme
in their need for staring down
everything, even the magnified
grass blades, greeny
rich shoots pushing up
through broken tarmac,
the vast invulnerabilities
of grass fought against
by the kindest of eyes but
eyes that talk trash & botch
things nonetheless. It
is morning, & it unfolds
like a letter from a father
to his startled, out-of-touch
daughter. She has everything
that anger has, anger
with its cold, bright view,
a roomful of windows
nailed shut—the rent due,
and late. What I have is a bird
this morning, a goldfinch,

I have this finch, singing,
not the slow squeaking
of the hinged door to
its cage as it is sprung,
freed. The door will open
soon, I feel sure.
                    I'm just
not into waiting actually.

What Really Happened Yesterday, Yesterday Will Never Know

Outside the cabin, a glove dropped years ago. The empty black calfskin skitters across the road, blown by a gust, & the tarmac seems to ripple & swell—like water pushed by wind on the river.

The man who stays in this cabin, his long marriage is over. Who is he now having been concealed after all by all that he seemed? A home...the marble coolness of the bathroom tiles on the soles of his feet in summer...trees on the street outside, their leaves rustling in the wind a signal to a barking dog—a city life, one house hidden behind another. Years ago, when they'd moved in, he & his wife had stripped the old, grimy wallpaper from all the rooms: lantern scenes of horse and buggy couples. They'd sanded the wide yellow pine on the floors—lots of dancing in the early years, parties that went on and on because everyone, all their friends, loved them. And he and his wife had loved the idea of their friends loving them.

Maybe he'd only wanted to stop living in his head: still thinks though. We always wanted to talk with each other, he thinks, then didn't. The fights, he still hears them, a kind of music about everything that can't be changed. Anger at breakfast, the stupidest start to the day. A love always in need of being fixed: jobs, money, the house, the two of them. The little brown moths visiting from some cruelty—poisonous in the things they'd say to each other.

But for what had appeared to be an entire earthly lifetime he'd loved being the father standing beneath a broken umbrella. For years, every year in the fall, on the sleeve of the sweatshirt that the man wore as he raked, there was always a single strand of his wife's long hair, dark brown going to silver: luck itself, the design revealed. Inside the house, on the dining room table, he could see his daughter's homework piled atop the books he was reading. He'd loved his wife's laughter in the wild wind at Dun Aengus, the two of them staring over the cliff edge on her birthday.

In the dream he'd had as his marriage was ending, just a moment or two after he'd locked the door to his old house for the last time, he'd met a friend on the street, near the maple tree that he'd planted when his daughter was born. Someone he hadn't seen for years, a dead man. "You know," he'd said to the friend, "I can't recall when I actually owned a house anymore." And his friend had laughed—"I'm glad you're finally having this experience," the dead one told him. He's almost sure that his friend was wearing two watches in the dream, one on each wrist: digital on the left, analog on the right—each of them set to a different hour.

And this man whose marriage is over now, where did he go then? Maybe he'd had to walk into something he wanted so badly to be the edge of a forest that it became the edge of a forest. Maybe he thought, "I won't be away for long." Oh, but he will be. He was.

Open & Shut

Then there was that elevator
as it rose toward
the 40th floor, & I could almost hear
in its mild bumping the music
a carriage full of courtiers from Anjou
might have had the pleasure of 300 years ago—
their dimwitted, duty-free faces
full of oysters & brandy,
with fields of vetch asters flowering by the dusty road,
a guiltless creaking of bossed leather & wind
whistling in the air.

Delinquency is a blessing
once in awhile…but only for those with souls
capable of being unbuttoned.

Orderliness threatens us constantly,
miserable with its confinement—
responsibility, achievement, reliability—

I'm just a working stiff now—
the kind of thought my father liked,
an inheritance, a supply chain.

What had happened to all those
solar flares I'd once imagined
to be pitching themselves from side to side
as they lit up my life like campfire?

Now my father has been dead a year—
he who carried both me & his feelings tight to his chest—

in this life, the wiry, strong body of a firefighter, & its shadow—
my father, who felt each of us
might be destroyed by weakness & need—

so: swagger, shrewdness, nerve,
that's what he liked, & drive; & coming home
to an abundant house he sought to lift his children.

He who holds you by a thread is not strong,
the thread is strong; so my brother
keeps telling me, all the way from Buenos Aires.

But only the world
and its news
could deliver on the back end
a truckload of bodies
to be autopsied tomorrow at a morgue in Gaza,
formerly boys smiling on a city beach,
killed by mortars—

they woke today, not thinking they would die.

My father—his firehouse nickname
was *Tiger*—my father asked
once that I never mention him again
in a book of poems—
"Do me a favor, will you?
leave me out of the rest."

Maybe he felt that poetry saves nobody—

was he wrong or right?

—an open question—

it's the window where
my mother hauls the laundry in—
my childhood clothesline,
its pulley wheel squealing—
it's my life, all of it.
This is *my* clothesline saga.

–for Noah Burton

Maria's Yellow Coat

I haven't had a lot of what
anyone would call
'sartorial smarts' in this life.

But outside the café
where Maria once sat
in her belted yellow long coat
there's an empty chair—
this wooden folding chair placed
under a sky as bewildered by the thought
of her savage yellow coat
as both me
and the weak, early December sun,
a sun that floats the way
Maria's knitted newsboy cap did once,
just above the horizon.

On the sidewalk
near this chair
lie a handful of mauled wing feathers,
plain gray & black feathers
not a single passerby
can step past
without staring. These strollers
seem surprised. Some
of them even stop to roll a quill or two
between thumb & index,
drifting off, a look of mild dismay
or concern on their faces—
the sound in their ears a heartbeat
their own

but nevertheless not exactly
like theirs, as if for that moment anyway
they held in their soft, dry hands
the living bird,
their heads bent close.

–for Charlie and Helen Simic

Fare Thee Well

Moss the carpet
underfoot makes a quiet shrine
beneath the birches & pines,

spectral trees, shadowy
as a biotech with no need
for venture cash—

the day demands an adolescent earth
to climb down to
on a ladder of blue spruce branches,

a high school landscape: woken on a chartered
bus in backwoods Vermont
coming home from a ski trip to Quebec,

I heard the young Jesuit
chaperones playing 'Age of Aquarius'
over the PA—

the sitar sound of a wild river
more beneficial at other moments
of my education.

What I wanted from women back then
wasn't always fucking exactly
but some belonging made of looks—

everything gets reified
by memories reshaped with the body
in mind,

an old shirt you could make paper from.
Her chin dimple quivering
when she adjusted a bra strap,

the lanky, pick-up game
precision of her walking over frozen slush
in knee-high boots. I feel kind of

Tecumseh Valley myself,
like Townes Van Zandt as a note
that reads 'fare thee well'

in a dead working girl's hand.
Everything, each incident, turns into a life,
whether wished for or not—

eight sugars in her prized cup of coffee—
remember our happiness? so simple?
sundered by a pint bottle of rye—

"Take your girlfriend
to get help," the priest said. "Me," she said,
"I'm just waiting for you

to check-out." Get with the work
a goat's heart knows best
in order to escape the bardo—

that's what someone else
would counsel later, neither enemy
nor ally.

White Givenchy

A fleeting bit of
memory is better forever than hope—
if you ask me.

If you ask the dead
whether or not they can be thanked,
you tend to get a response
courteous in its dexterity, but bitter & annoying
for how it greets you once & for all
with silence;

it leaves you stuck there in the rain,
your big, bald scalloper's head
soaked to the brim
by a sequence of disclosures, sad stains
arrived from everywhere at once—

the dead will teach their silence
to all us unbelievers—

here comes a quick salutation
from my brown-eyed carouser,
my laughing lost & found,
she who'd gone with me down to Tompkins Park
so that we could eat falafel
from a particular yellow pushcart,
(now, *that* was grace—
the innate care
with which she held the dripping rollup
at a distance
from her oyster silk blouse,

some sleeveless, consignment-shop Givenchy
with pearlescent buttons—
ducking her head & leaning over to bite
decisively into the soft pita).
I remember how she'd showered
and shaved 3-days worth of stubble
from her armpits
before putting on that blouse.
She hated plaids—
thought the wearers
benighted, needy…clownish
as any knob-kneed, bark-shedding scion
of a river birch
standing crooked in an empty autumn field.

I don't say that it's all right
to go under, but it may be the only way
through this life.

Anger Thinks, So Anger Thinks

Tony, there's no Freud
in this feud, just brother hate
without the theory
to grace it—
muddy water boiling at a moody clip.

The younger brother thinks
the older a bore,
tho a genius of sorts
(kerneled in his brain
are all those popcorn opinions
he brims with,
his "work product,"
the ideas he upsells
like baby strollers renovated
into space capsules);

the younger's a motormouth
and narcissist
(according to the elder), misled
by reality (according to his brother)
the way a bottle
blond is misled by the mirror
she holds in her hand.

Hugging each other at night
before falling asleep in their bed, these brothers
they're like the salt crystals
that the ice leaves on a street as it melts,
residues of pattern
shaped like elegant rosettes,

rosettes that turn out
to have been fashioned on anvils,
a high-carbon steel
forged by anger—

go ahead,
smash a hammer on those feelings
as much as you wish,
they won't care.
I'm here to stay, anger thinks,
I'll live in your head,
the floor at the top of the house
where all the heat goes to die.

Whatever Did You Say?

Laughter is close too, even if it is
just the *schadenfreude*

of middle-school girls,
their juicy, eye-rolling, malicious

glee flying
down the street (like a tiny pink slug

in a pigeon's beak), hotting up
the air—why pretend

you can't hear? Laughter,
the only eternity

that's real. Laughter
and its toothy

lift off, even
when toxic. "Save me"

is what's written
on the faces of so many

passing strangers,
"save me" & "fuck you."

So the ancient Tibetan *arhats*
teach, focused as they are

by the incense of sage
and the wailing of toddlers

near a septic tank—
a thousand years dead

these masters,
but still thinking

they're fast asleep
in their boyhood beds.

Our Words

Our words as it were muted
like the throwdown of a summer hailstorm we'd heard once
so long ago & then again
last night two whiskies to the west of the ardent esplanade
even if it was only a feeling
a surge beatific & stony took place as we sat there listening
on the high stools of The Sevens Ale House
the two graybeards near us speaking quietly then
of the benefits of cognitive therapy
in time their words not ours
burbling under the auspices of the surfer guitars
piped softly through the bar
and given power as I surely must have guessed
by those thick black cables
that a line crew had run to The Sevens
from a diesel down the block,
a portable power generator
graded industrial-class
by the word *Grief*
tagged on its hood in graffiti—
that bill of lading
signed sealed delivered:
Grief Grief Grief—the name
of some would-be neighborhood warlord
written in reverb.

Feelings are full, rich, they open vast
and did so always
if you can believe it, it was like
the two of us were just getting to know each other again
but even so I was telling you how my life would end

before my work did, which was true for you too
you said—we'd each planned it that way—
otherwise maybe we'd been friends
a thousand wavering northern days already
and chatterboxing the whole way
listening for whatever bread & cheese advice
we might have had for each other
in the love that unfolds
into mutual understanding seemingly by chance
we agreed that everyone we respected
at some point had had to invent a code of conduct
for themselves,
and soon we would too,
soon enough.

Years went by tho of course they had to
going where years go ill-conceived & flashing
and then back from Paris
honeycombed & ironclad
you came bringing news
kept alive by the sad black quarter horses of Zurich
news of our beloved long-dead teachers
news that travels as they did whenever possible
like foxes running swiftly
over dead autumn leaves on leathery paws
drifting over leaves that
in spring were yellow-going-to-green—
now that we are almost old too, you said,
almost as old as our teachers were once,
they will not bite us—
they're coming to lick us clean.

—for Stuart Dischell

Steve

Another word is *heartsick*,
Steve. As it was when I stood
at the podium I'd been given,
the crowd before me growing,
those listeners I took to be
my cousins…their heads,
their anonymous, truant heads
filled to the brim with spaces
unimaginable to wind. I'd rather
bring a word to Steve, I thought…
Steve, who I'd brought so
many words to once. Steve,
the least dead thing the dead
have ever seen. *Bring a word
to each of your cousins*—this
was what the messenger had asked
in the hour right before dawn—
*weakness isn't defect, but fear of
weakness is.* A woman had appeared
then…if appeared is what
I really mean. For a long time
after she'd unbuttoned her jacket
I'd sat there in the grassy yard
trying hard to feel alone. I wasn't tho.
I knew because I'd touched
the purple silk, the silk lining
her grandmother had sewn
for her father, who had given her
the jacket. *Go ask the cousins*—
that is what the night manager
had advised. Then, without warning,

everything was moving forward,
save for the man who shivered there
while motoring backward
in his wheelchair as it rained.
Steve could have figured it out,
I know. He could explain it to me.
Still wishing Steve were alive—
someone to tell it all to today.
The last Steve left to tell.

The Wave

And trying as you need me
to keep it simple I can tell you
that the bees were able
at all times to pass safely
through the glass, their wings
rubbing briskly if needed
as they moved from one side
of the window to the other,
though the store sold appliances
not honey—used refrigerators
and stoves mostly—so it was
odd to begin with, that hive,
and in any case no one could
recall anymore why the grandfather
long dead had installed it
in the storefront when he'd opened
for business, its combs dark as
cribs alive with swarm—dark wax,
and the darker honey dotted
by vast, tilted galaxies of pollen—
a tunnel connected a hole
cut in the glass to the hive,
a tube of transparent plastic
three or four inches in diameter
big enough that the bees
could pass as they wished—
but touch your fingers
to that window & in its vibrations
you would feel a warmth
flowing slowly up your arm
and as if within hearing distance

of your breathing just then
often enough it seemed a bee
would emerge from the tunnel
by itself, a completeness of one,
hovering, testing the air—
and after a while as you stood there
it'd feel like watching a woman
as she steps into lapping waves—
low tide, the labyrinth of granite
slabs she'd navigated through
the tide pools behind her now,
open sand beneath her feet,
the ocean a part of her day
she walks into cold water
in an old, aquamarine two-piece,
guided by something invisible
to clarity itself, some part of her
secret self—it feels good
to have the ocean in her hair,
restoring—pale skin, some
freckles, legs that seem to go
all the way to the sky
because the point of view
you watch her from is that
of a single spiny sea urchin
hugged to a rock below—
you'd been thrust into this life
you felt—for so long you'd felt
as if it rose up before you
like a wall, solid, immoveable…
but you began to understand…
it's much more intimate
than that…nothing is solid…
you exist in the thoughts of

others as much as you do
in your own, the thoughts
of all those who saw you,
even if, like this woman,
it was only once—she'd glanced
at you in town the day before
while riding her bike—
she was holding the top
of her blouse with her left hand,
the fingertips of her right
steering the handlebar
lightly—a button had popped
loose from the blouse—
and she was a little cold
but awake now—salt
of a wave on her lip. Trust me.
The wave is not the water,
the water only tells us
that the wave is going by.

The Believer

And so you make your approach,
you make a beeline at the fair grounds
for a real attention-getter, something like a biker
in baggy camo pants—
two eyes tattooed to the back of his shaved skull—
eyes of stone-cold
detachment, eyes that can see
how you go to him
for cheap advice. It's dangerous,
tho not for you. Impetuousness,
yours—bright, swift, sure—
it moistens everything.
You're the one who knows enough
to pray. Here comes the water,
you told me once, a clerk
in the waterworks when I was sent there
to be brought to my knees.
I'm almost with you now too,
here at the end of the harvest fair
the binding shadows of poplar & birch
casting a cool net
above the screaming & blinking of all those
tossed by the tilt-a-whirl. No wonder
the crows called to each other last week,
constantly re-setting
the boundaries of this field,
guarding against all the shaking
and laughter to come.
I was almost there with them too.
It's as if for so long
my whole life has revolved around trying

to judge the perfect point
to say hello. I was even almost
there at the top of the stairs
when your mother went on screaming
in the rain. Now your mother & her guilt
out of all that is left
sits down before a window
to gaze upon the delicate play
of a life set loose,
your life. And crows,
well, you've heard of
crows. Heard of them.
To make room for air
in his chest when he cries a crow
has to hunch his wings
and breathe deep,
in the field-green heat
a shrub of blue-black feathers
shrugging. Crows. They cry for quiet.
And it is quiet,
as though a pregnant woman
had tugged a sheer
summer dress over her rounded belly,
and come to stand here,
almost hidden.

Sundial Seeking Sun

So much to listen for I thought
        in the midst of one of those
moments of sparrow-like sadness
        tho no self-respecting sparrow
would agree as apparently I had
        to take up with Hardy's lessons
in sorrow having to put on tweed
        camp clothes & set out for a solitary
tramp in wind-blown rain not desperate
        so much as stoic while forlorn
all that religion of an old-timey sort
        proud of every passing thought
like a prisoner who mistakes his cell
        for a throne when in fact
the only thing I had wanted after all
        was for her to tell me more
about the photo of Sid's truck
        parked as I'd thought it had been
in Kelvington Saskatchewan for so long
        that's the water tower in the background
as common as wheat on the Sask horizon
        but no one small-town sings
of the greenness in green eyes anymore
        do they & because the eyes
are a borderline not to be crossed sometimes
        someone has to tremble
on the other side of a table & you
        you on your side have to sit there
doing nothing but listening & watching
        surprised by how much you didn't know
after all it's nobody's business
        if a secret wanted to feel protected

it was for the best so I just sat there silent
        because when a ghost returns
to the neighborhood a little emaciated
        and pawing through a pocketbook
for some object she can't think of
        the name for your chemistry alters
often almost imperceptibly & without
        at all understanding exactly how
you let yourself become the one loved
        the one loved enough to be told
that for years after her sister had died
        her mother kept on buying toys & clothes
appropriate to the age her sister
        had been the year of her death
gifts that had to be accepted
        so no I did not get up & offer her
my coat & it wouldn't have stopped
        her trembling anyway it's true
because what you owe someone
        is the space to feel what they sometimes
feel now & then when speaking
        brave naked a little more real.

The Hinge

February's basket-case sunset—
fading embers
when the fire grows cold—
when it seems at last
that you're likely to reap
every cold-blooded & wicked thing you've
ever sown at the proton level;
but this is a twice-lived life—
once in the heart,
then again in the brain
(or vice-versa);
that's just how it is,
how, inevitably, it just seems to be
April one day,
the 'platitudes of our discontent' fading,
our hoof prints in icy slush faded,
our Home County woolens dry-cleaned
and folded in memere's cedar chest,
the snow-squalls no longer a roof to live beneath,
all that *schmutzfinke* in the gutters
giving way to a warm drizzle—
the mist gathers like the mesmer
around an accordion & violin—
April the hinge between
feral winter / feral spring,
the tart, citron color
of the willows,
a yellowish-green
seeping through their long branches
at the same steady rate
as the rain coming down

and stippling the puddles.
Not an ounce of vanity to any of it,
that's how it looks from here—
listen to me,
it's like when a dolphin
swims up to you & lets you touch
its side…you have
no idea…

After a Certain Phone Call
When Nothing Changed
And Everything Was Different

After the rain had fallen lightly for awhile
        on the road to the old steamboat landing
tho I'd been too confused to notice I knew
        having to get said what I had to say like a man
one who was having a heart attack
        in his brain the sounds of the words scattering
into the shredded shapes of dead flowers
        mostly marigolds & carnations & something
of an ugly whitish color cast onto those waters
        baffled enough already by how ocean meets river
at that spot where I like to sit & suddenly I was
        silent no possible explanation no explanation
adequate or even implausible forthcoming
        and no forwarding address for the answer
I thought maybe would arrive late after all
        and you had laughed gently & with kindness
(tho you were hurting when you spoke)
        you said "you're still trying to do the math"
meaning I might want to stop
        my attempts to solve all the doubts
both mine & yours by multiplying them
        endlessly a doorway to all we couldn't know
having opened in that silence & as the miles
        we talked across dissolved
it was as if you stood close I could feel you then
        your breath on my cheek the warm rain
falling again in light drops the traces
        of something that could be loved
without anyone having to make it whole.

Oh

How long? How long
will it be that I
get to feel this, this golden orb
pinging in my heart?
—a sleepless 3 a.m.
as right & wrong as air
now that the bug-spray mingles there
with Bach. So much
vibrato in the viola now
that the overwhelmed note
has to hide in my head,
bumping lightly
against some thoughts, nudging
one: you know
how I'd like to lick the spot
on your neck where you so often
rub that scent I love?—
well, maybe you don't—
but if I were dying
yours would be the last face
I would want at the end
to see. The archer
elegant & serene in posture & stretch pants
who brings gifts both
kind & painful when she reminds you
you have a heart.
                    In the dark
I had been trying for a while to get at it,
what it meant
when you wrote. Maybe
I could be the hero of the story

however it went. I am not
the hero of the story. I'm only a man who
a year ago woke from a dream
and heard a voice, a voice asking
the one thing he needed to be asked:
"what makes you think you
can't be touched in your life?"
I don't mean to say
that I think it was your voice
I heard, only it is
so much like the things you do say
that I want to believe
it must have been you.

Wild Strawberries

Tiny wild strawberries
in the uncut grass—a tartness
that vibrates the tongue
more than a flavor—
how can I quiet my
mind if there isn't any
stillness in them?
                    There is the story
I keep telling myself—there is
always that—& there is the story
I might hear, if I were to listen,
if I could just stand here,
silent.
            Tho another thing
I have waited a long time to hear
is the galloping of hooves
in the dark.
                    Well, born with a brain,
die with a brain. But a certain
miracle seems to survive regardless—
beach plums: the *rosa*
rugosa wear mercurochrome
on their lapels. A heavy bush
of them curling like a wave
full of the scent of soulful solid heat—
sunlight siphons it from the earth
like a pump, just as it did
behind my grandfather's camp,
wherever that marsh was exactly
and whoever I was already
when I was that boy

who could have written this poem
if he'd wanted to.
                        It's hard to keep
track of it all
if your brain is embarrassed
by having been born
in a body.
              So, thanks—
thank you for
making my heartbeat
faster just now.

Reinventions

We only wanted
to be seen. The world too
wants to be looked at,
but what popped into sight
just now was evil—
a pipeline carrying crude
full of extinctions, chokeholds
and pepper spray, those
crimes against humanity
the torturers & theological
bankers have thought
up, the pro-lifers
who kill at long-distance
by drone, jailers of
children. Look at that
tho—all by itself a book
can heat a cold classroom
like a snake with
one benevolent ball of
fire in its mouth—
look at that, the world
could say but doesn't.
That's a huge willow
over there as well, a savior
for all its reinventions
of shade. Every cardinal
calling from a tree
assumes the world
is hard of hearing too;
the world hears whatever
it wants. Did I really say,

"a warring of the safest furs
is stouter than a gem?"
No—I said, a wavering of
the softest fern is louder
than a jet: roar of the arrived,
of the departing. The two of us
have been speaking
of someone whose
mother had lost her hearing
in the course of giving
birth to her, from then on
declining gradually
into grief & isolation.
We're standing
across from the Oddfellows
Hall & the lampshade
shop, by the side of the road
clipping hydrangea
and Queen Anne's lace,
chamomile. I'll just say it
again: *chamomile*.

Eyes Closed, Rye Beach

Around now
the sun's high enough
in this place we both love that the wood thrush
across the road has gone silent.
Not that it's under any illusions—
no wood thrush
(so far as we know) has ever once believed
(or needed to believe) that its singing
had lifted the sun, even if it is possible it did.
And the sun is high enough here
that the beach is full
of allowances for everything
its children ask
(everything, that is, except nudity)—
tho without swimsuit
Amy has walked into the water
in her expensive bra,
and afterwards her cut-offs
will be bettered
because the sea has made them softer
with its saltiness
and all that rubbing I can
see with my eyes closed because
I can hear the waves
breaking.
        Any one of us can see
with our ears if we want—
but no one should try too hard—
ego isn't in it—tho a hunger for mercies might be:
        my marriage is over
now—my father has been dead

five years—Tony has died,
without a word—the hooded child
lags farther & farther behind, startled,
out-of-touch—and I am not the one
who knows to pray—
          all those bits & pieces
of a story I brought with me to Amy.
                              When Amy comes back
from her swim it's almost the ocean
that presses its wet palm against my forehead—
cold, reliable, grinding, restorative—
but in the gear whine of two motorcycles racing
a half-mile away
I see us passing once more
into the safekeeping of Shaker bees
as we walked the hillside yesterday
below those dormitories no one goes to any longer
for sleep. The pollen of thousands
of pine trees powdered across
the greenest leaves there, the yellow-white stipple
of dots I'd wiped my thumb over
while passing. "*Snowflake Appaloosa*
is the loveliest phrase," the guide had said
as she stood in the doorway
to the apiary like a password. I thought that too
of course. The yellow streak of my thumb
across Amy's palm. We'd just left
the stables. I thought that
yesterday. Still do.

By Then

By then I was leaving,
and the deer in the meadow had stopped
paying me their mind. I was alone
as I'd always been
but twice as deep for knowing it
now. Sometimes it's OK
you have to wander a strange house
covered only by a blanket,
itchy wool rubbing against your naked ass
and shoulders—
the coarse gray fire station blanket
given me as a child. I didn't know
whether this was one of those
times; I mean,
I didn't know if I was "OK."
Shame thinks of us
in friendly terms—it sees how we are,
on the blink—it wants only
to do us the kindness
of anchoring us to the world it makes us
feel unworthy of.
I kept thinking a good cry
will take care of everything
wrong—getting
day by day
skinnier but filled
somehow despite it all
to bursting.
Do me a favor,
I wanted to ask shame,

hold me, why don't you?
Because at heart
it's just that simple
maybe. I wanted to be
held, that's all. When I say
the word "world"
I mean love of course.
When I say "then"
I mean now. Always.

ACKNOWLEDGEMENTS

Earlier versions of these poems appeared in various locations, sometimes with other titles. My thanks to the editors of *Big Bell, the Brooklyn Rail, Four Way Review, Plume, Salamander*, and *Tuesday; An Art Project*.

"The Wish of Those Who Named Us" appeared originally as part of the Academy of American Poets' Poem-a-Day project (with the title "Strictly Speaking").

This book was ferried into the light of day with the help of many hands. Thank you, friends: Peter Behrens, David Blair, Noah Burton, Maria Chelko, Olena Kalytiak Davis, Stuart Dischell, Mark Gosztyla, David Guenette, Fred Marchant, Katie Peterson, Candice Reffe, Simone Rivard, Amy Sauber, Charles Simic, Tom Sleigh, and Sarah Stickney.

The river this book floats on was brought into being by another friend, Askold Melnyczuk—neither the river or the book would be here without his enthusiasm and hard work. Thanks to him for his push, and to Ezra Fox and everyone else at Arrowsmith Press for all their efforts at guiding it along.

All gratitude to Jeesoo Lee for making the image on the cover of this book and permitting its use, and for the invention, soulfulness and wit that is in her art and friendship.

Photo by Amy Sauber

David Rivard is the author of six previous books, including *Standoff*, *Sugartown*, *Wise Poison*, and *Torque*. His work has won the PEN/ New England Prize in poetry, the James Laughlin Prize from the Academy of American Poets, and the Agnes Lynch Starrett Poetry Prize, and he has been a finalist for the *Los Angeles Times* Book Prize. Among his other honors are fellowships from the Guggenheim Foundation, the National Endowment for the Arts, the Civitella Ranieri Foundation, and the Fine Arts Work Center in Provincetown. In 2006, he was given the O.B. Hardison Poetry Prize by the Folger Shakespeare Library in recognition of both his writing and teaching. He lives on the coast of Maine.

Books by
ARROWSMITH
PRESS

Girls by Oksana Zabuzhko

Bula Matari/Smasher of Rocks by Tom Sleigh

This Carrying Life by Maureen McLane

Cries of Animal Dying by Lawrence Ferlinghetti

Animals in Wartime by Matiop Wal

Divided Mind by George Scialabba

The Jinn by Amira El-Zein

Bergstein
edited by Askold Melnyczuk

Arrow Breaking Apart by Jason Shinder

Beyond Alchemy by Daniel Berrigan

Conscience, Consequence: Reflections on Father Daniel Berrigan
edited by Askold Melnyczuk

Ric's Progress by Donald Hall

Return To The Sea by Etnairis Rivera

The Kingdom of His Will by Catherine Parnell

Eight Notes from the Blue Angel by Marjana Savka

Fifty-Two by Melissa Green

Music In—And On—The Air by Lloyd Schwartz

Magpiety by Melissa Green

Reality Hunger by William Pierce

Soundings: On The Poetry of Melissa Green
edited by Sumita Chakraborty

The Corny Toys by Thomas Sayers Ellis

Black Ops by Martin Edmunds

Museum of Silence by Romeo Oriogun

City of Water by Mitch Manning

Passeggiate by Judith Baumel

Persephone Blues by Oksana Lutsyshyna

The Uncollected Delmore Schwartz
edited by Ben Mazer

The Light Outside by George Kovach

The Blood of San Gennaro by Scott Harney
edited by Megan Marshall

No Sign by Peter Balakian

Firebird by Kythe Heller

The Selected Poems of Oksana Zabuzhko
edited by Askold Melnyczuk

The Age of Waiting by Douglas J. Penick

Manimal Woe by Fanny Howe

Crank Shaped Notes by Thomas Sayers Ellis

The Land of Mild Light by Rafael Cadenas
edited by Nidia Hernández

The Silence of Your Name by Alexandra Marshall

Flame in a Stable by Martin Edmunds

Mrs. Schmetterling by Robin Davidson

This Costly Season by John Okrent

Thorny by Judith Baumel

ARROWSMITH is named after the late William Arrowsmith, a renowned classics scholar, literary and film critic. General editor of thirty-three volumes of *The Greek Tragedy in New Translations*, he was also a brilliant translator of Eugenio Montale, Cesare Pavese, and others. Arrowsmith, who taught for years in Boston University's University Professors Program, championed not only the classics and the finest in contemporary literature, he was also passionate about the importance of recognizing the translator's role in bringing the original work to life in a new language.

Like the arrowsmith who turns his arrows straight and true,
a wise person makes his character straight and true.

— Buddha